GW00500335

NO RETURN GAME

First published in 2013
The Dedalus Press
13 Moyclare Road
Baldoyle
Dublin 13
Ireland

www.dedaluspress.com

Copyright © Tom Mathews, 2013

ISBN 978 1 906614 75 1

All rights reserved.
No part of this publication may be reproduced in any form or
by any means without the prior permission of the publisher.

Dedalus Press titles are represented in the UK by
Central Books, 99 Wallis Road, London E9 5LN
and in North America by Syracuse University Press, Inc.,
621 Skytop Road, Suite 110, Syracuse, New York 13244.

Cover image credit:
ESO/M.-R. Cioni/VISTA Magellanic Cloud survey.
Acknowledgment: Cambridge Astronomical Survey Unit
Printed in Ireland by Gemini International Ltd.

The Dedalus Press receives financial assistance from
The Arts Council / An Chomhairle Ealaíon

NO RETURN GAME

Tom Mathews

DEDALUS PRESS
DUBLIN, IRELAND

ACKNOWLEDGEMENTS

Acknowledgements are due to the editors of the following in which a number of these poems, or versions of them, originally appeared: *Crannog, Cyphers, The Moth, Poetry Ireland Review, The SHOp* and *The Stinging Fly.*

There is no return game
between a man and his stars.
— Samuel Beckett, *Murphy*

for Marion Kelly
and Sara O'Rourke

Contents

Notice How My Hands Never Leave My Wrists

The poet as magician.
There's a phrase
To conjure with.
Yeats dressed as Merlin, smiling through Celtic mist
Of lapis lazuli and amethyst.
Blake's angels dance before your very eyes.
Eliot is Dumbledore, muggle-disguised.
Auden in evening dress and gloves
Machine guns gags,
Filling the public square with doves,
The stage with flags,
And ending with a song.
What super troopers.
Most of my tricks go wrong
Like Tommy Cooper's.

But poems, like rabbits hidden in a hat,
Sometimes appear by magic. Just like that!

Editorial

When you make cuts
Cut deep for preference.
Say what you mean.
Find the mot juste.
Delete the reference.
Don't come the Marcel Proust.
Come clean;
A poem's a love machine.
Poems should tighten the nuts.

Champagne

for Bill Doyle

'The shutter coming down,' said Cartier
Bresson, 'is the descending guillotine.'
Love's aide memoire, Daguerre's memorious mirror.

Arresting transience of kiss or dance
Ironically now, your flesh-made-ash
Accords their evanescence permanence.

You froze the traffic, stilling crowds and cars,
F-stopping down to halt the horse's gallop.
Without the night we cannot see the stars.
Pictures of days need darkness to develop.

Your world was made of images. No words
Remain. A life is there in black and white.
Though time erases what the sun records
You touch us with your still available light.

St. Patrick's Day

The chill wind ripples March-wet grass
As virtuous from early mass
Incurious the cyclists pass
The poet reading in the sun

Of one whose dreams and hopes and fears
Are water flowing by the weirs,
But one man turns away in tears
Before the reading's done

Who will not hear Liam Brady
Play his violin again
At Kavanagh's bench, by the Grand Canal
On St. Patrick's Day, in the rain.

Canal

A swan stands up applauding in the dark
Caught on my mobile phone.
I think about the lion of St. Mark
Clapping his wings of stone.

Two Poems from the Irish of Aifric Mac Aodha

1.

Two moons shake
On the aquaface,
A lane through brake
Is going no place.

The soft wind soughs,
The leaf-nets move,
Leaves hooked on boughs
Sway in a grove.

A shadow-blight
Through the lake is stealing,
A water sprite
Its web concealing.

And what odds anyway
Your own kidnap
If a silkie woman
Might a God entrap.

Your voice new-risen
No woman's resembling,
In its narrow prison
Exulting and trembling.

2.

The swan will escape
From her shadow's rill
And leave her tear shape
On the grassy hill.

Her bright bride-price
Will the butterfly quench
And bend with his rainbow
A little dead branch;

And the antic spume
Disperse and dim
To droplets shimmering
On the dark brim;

Your dancing too
Lose all its grace
And your gamin limbs
Come to age apace;

No guards for Syrinx
But the reeds and ferns,
Tall spearsmen, phalanx
Of mud-grey kerns.

A.M.D.G

This April morning, moorhen,
I'm glad to see you glide
Along the sunny grand canal
On your black backside.

Where the water willows lean
Down from the lawns
You navigate a deeper green
Among the sleepy swans,

And bring me so much happiness
The busy city's sound recedes
A moment from my consciousness
Until you vanish in the reeds.

Mnemosyne

Scarlet anemones in humid pools
Contracting and expanding like a lung,
Far out to sea the dolphins in their schools
Break water. Watching, he again is young.

Remembering a landscape and a tryst,
A sundering upon a distant shore,
The longships' prows emerging from the mist,
A snowflake melting on a blackened oar.

Mountainous, numinous, unseen,
Cold as the stars that she reflects
The shattering translucent green
Totters and melts and resurrects
The thousand things that might have been,
The single thing he recollects.

The Legacy

Profaned the rose,
Leafless the chestnut tree,
Toppled the tower he loved.
What hole was left in the sea,
The bloody fist removed?

What was diminished, what improved?
What made, and what destroyed?
What given to eternity
But kisses to the void?

No Lasting City

Irish bards, my kin and kith,
Older than Troy, older than Troy,
Ceded Yeats a cache of myth
Older than Troy.

Lines I write for you are lies
Older than Troy, older than Troy,
But something moves behind your eyes
Older than Troy.

Need

Youth have you and laughter and sensation.
I, only need.
O dark haired beauty it is my lamentation
That you pay me no heed.

Something New

How many heads
Will your head turn?
As many sticks
As a fire can burn.

Pulse of your wrist
Was all my song;
Ice in the fist
Endures as long.

The Singing Tree

Your love? I thought as soon to see
A princess poor, a singing tree.
I made a tree of words for you.
Those leaves were birds that sang and flew.

In its bare branches none remain.
The sky grows darker. In the rain
Now underneath that silent tree
A ragged princess comes to me.

Memorare

If I evoked a look's caress
Because a zephyr raised my dress
That was the wind's affair.

Or if a petal's loveliness
Rested a moment on a tress
That was the flower's.

And if my eyes were wild and bright,
As were the little waves that night,
That was the stars'.

But when, as now in after years,
My eyes would fill with sudden tears,
Ah, that was ours.

Sail Away

A fleece of gold, hung in a tree,
Drew Jason's men across a sea.
And Argo's prow cleft Colchis' mist
When all the sea was amethyst.

Oh all the sea was grey the night
We sailed for London Town
But your hair was bright as a fleece of gold
When the rain dropped its diamonds down.

Mensa

Flame is to icicle
False is to true
Fish is to bicycle
As I am to you

Rain is to runnel
Star is to sea
Love is to tunnel
As you are to me

Joy is to sorrow
Wait is to bus
Time is to tomorrow
As love is to us.

Bedspring Music

Shed the sheets, discard the duvet,
Cast aside the borrowed Banville.
Moister than a weepie movie's
Rochester's receptive anvil.

A pink-lined purse, an ace of spades
Whose liquid assets lie displayed.
An itching tickle in the curls,
A clyster irrigated pearl.

Blind digits scan the scrotal braille,
Bright lactic fireworks flash and fail.
Tsunami tremors fade to spray,
Dry beige as bone or white as day.

And tongue athirst advances slow
Through axial russet. Afterglow.

After Donne

Would you know a ladye's minde
T'were easier go counte the starres,
Freeze summer sunne with winter winde,
Dissuade all principalities from warres.

Yette I doe thinke where reason most aboundeth
Some fewe founde out this art.
But he the Theban sphinx herself confoundeth
Who truly findeth out hys ladye's hearte.

Found in a Drawer with Two Rings

Cold jewels slumber ever in the earth,
Warm seeds a richer emerald put forth,
Dull rubies' fires smould'ring out of sight
Flare forth in flowers spring's soft rains ignite.

No precious stone engraved by slow degrees
Can half so precious be as hours like these.
All our eternity's but night to noon
Whose names are writ on other stones too soon.

The comet's omen in a moment flies,
The glow worm's spark's no sooner lit than dies.
But diamond polished to transparency
Will not outlast this brief fidelity.

Doctor Field

'They say transposing your words means you want to have sex with the person you're talking to,' she said.

'Ha ha.' I replied. 'Dr. Field would have a Freud day with that.'

The Two Traditions

She reads a snow poem
From the Chinese of Li Po.
I eat a Kung Po duckling
From the Chinese of Tony Choy.

'Conundra'

Who, looking at the cloud
Conceives the thunder's clamour,
Foresees the lightning hurled?
But shepherds learn the weather
As cobblers learn leather,
As a child learns the world.

Who, looking at the peacock's egg
Envisages the feather,
The hundred eyes unfurled?
So we, lying together,
Each round the other curled,
Begin to learn each other
As a child learns the world.

Ending Up

We who were so in love in May
Find we have little now to say
So sit and stare at Galway Bay.

Though moonlight tries to look romantic
And our shadows move gigantic
In the candlelit café

We little speak as monks in cloisters,
On our plates untasted oysters
By lees of chardonnay remain.

Neath lobster pots and copper kettles
Across a bouquet's fallen petals
Your green eyes sting my heart like nettles

As it settles in to rain.

Song

Hungover, drunk, in the rain.
She's ignored my calls
Since 9.15.
A star falls.
I wish the moon was Solpadeine.

The End of the Affair

"At least say something."
But she turned away.
And so said everything there was to say.

Topsy Says

"When I die
Have them cut me open, do.
And you'll see how full of love
I was for you."

Aw Topsy.

Arts Club Drunk

He holds himself with Henry James'
Vinegar aplomb.
And smiling from his eyes exclaims
'My darling, I was dropping names
Before they dropped the bomb.'

Jean Cocteau in a cocktail bar
Après un film noir
Giggling like a gigolo
Called me his 'Petit matelot'.
And you know what sailors are.

In days like these, of times like those
My heart's too full to speak,
When Gertrude read me out her 'Rose',
When Eliot admired my prose,
And Ezra praised my greek.

This Just In

Trieste.
Madman writes book.

Portora.
Headmaster erases pervert's initials.

Paris.
Godot named as pilot. Playwright leaves plane.

Dublin.
Myles, five, sees city burn.

Madrid.
'What d'you hope to see here Mr Behan?'
'Franco's funeral.'

"One for the Master"

The speaker being a Princeton co-ed, the word 'Bad' is to be considered in the demotic American sense: cool, sexually attractive.

Odi et amo, ever since we met, and yet, Armagh
      virumque cano.
Grey, owlish, celtic, charming, a romantic,
And once I heard him speak
And tried to spell
My way through his critiques
(His marking is perhaps a tad pedantic).
My knees were weak
And so I fell.
Bad about the Moy, grand, and Saville-Row clad,
Or bare as Cupid, he's so bad about the Moy
I guess I'm stupid.
All the daydreams that I've had about the boy
And when they put my author on the stage
He breaks a heart with each New Yorker page.
Though people call him a flaneur
He knows his shopping list from Schopenhauer, I'm sure
There's just a touch of Count de Sade about the boy.
If I'm 'an amadawn'
What do I care?
Look in the Bangor pawnshop of his heart,
You'll find me there.
He reads from 'Quoof' and gives that goofy grin.
And poof! I'm Pangur Bán upon a hot tin roof again.
I'm glad I signed up for this discipline.
And though I know that it's absurd
To spend my evenings looking up his words,
It's just that he's so bad about the Moy.

Mr Larkin's Sunday Morning Insomnia

That was Mr Heaney's room
I almost blundered into.
Too many gins.
Three a.m. and nauseous.
Let's wheel out old mortality again.
(Oh merde, all must be interred.)
No, not tonight.
Why should I let der tod death squat on my life?
When first there's hurt
To be endured, sick as Flaubert
Of masturbating my exhausted head
To make the phrases spurt.
In the mind's attic
First the libido dies
And when the gift dies too
What muse-distilled Viagra can revive
The flaccid Vatic?
Not all those jazzmags, no
Nor all that jazz.
Gin from the mini bar then
Tepid in the toothmug
Tasting of Euthymol.
Bed.

I should have been an enervate Bostonian
Mingling the metaphysicians with Laforgue.
A thunderclap,
A flash scores the sky's lead.
Not much poetry in Motion.
Movement.
As good a name as any, I'd have said,
For a load of crap.

Brasserie Lipp

Genet kissed me when we met.
I was talking soupe au gratin
With the Beaver, chic as yet
In a little skirt of satin.

Who am I? Why, Jean Paul Sartre,
A sad old existentialist, me.
One thing soothes my weary heart:
Genet kissed me.

W.H. Auden's 'Humpty Dumpty'

Smash all the timers, let the sands run out,
Prevent the concert in the last redoubt.
Cancel the papers, put the Rolls up on blocks,
Replace the king's men and his horses in their box.

Print the announcement in the Times with black edges,
Bid the herd cease its sighing in the sedges,
Strip down each blossom from the apple bough;
Cause the wall to be dismantled, he will not need it now.

He was my prose, my verse, my lines, my words.
He was my rose tree full of singing birds.
He was my tortoise in his jewelled shell.
I thought he'd sit on walls forever; but he fell.

Melt all the icecaps, suck the oceans dry.
Burn every copy of 'The Egg and I';
Uncover your head and cower in the freezing rain.
For nobody now can put him back together again.

Sweeney In Loco Parentis

A polaroid this morning mild
In Sweeney's post. Her smile is bland.
'You are the father of my child.'
Flutters from his unconscious hand.

Arising from her sleep in Dorset
The Canton lady it depicts
Forces her form into a corset
Constricting as the snake constricts

And seated on the unmade bed
Considering the time it takes
Draws on a pair of tights instead
Of stockings shed like skins of snakes,

Consults the clock. Her time is brief,
Her toilet at the best perfunctory.
Stocking in lieu of handkerchief
Effects the office of emunctory.

Sweeney, recovered from his swoon,
Hastens to keep their luncheon date.
Time's hand is at the prick of noon,
The girl unfashionably late.

Distrait as he eviscerates
The bowl of moules he eats for two,
Crocodile-sob reiterates
The question: 'What are we to do?'

Sweeney aborts the pregnant pause
By passage of ignoble gas.
The lobsters fumble hobbled claws
Impotent in their cloudy glass

Prison, hard by the Gentlemans.
Their ancestors in water clear
Had fed upon Sir Patrick Spens
And Scottish lairds off Inisheer.

Images dull as Logie Baird's
Set thoughts of heavier tanks astir,
Crushed asians in Tiananmen Square,
In Sweeney's mind diffuse and blur.

The Oriental from the Ladies,
Returning smiles, takes Sweeney's arm,
Consigns her menstrual flow to Hades,
For all has proved a false alarm.

Blues for the Captain

You made a midnight creep,
Slipped the leash,
Stole my stash,
Shaved off my moustache.
I strike a match
In the pumpkin patch,
Stumble back,
Lift the latch.
What you said in the note
Make me dream when I can't sleep,
Make me itch where I can't scratch.

Ivor Cutler

Your slightness made you great. The amazing thing
About you was how ordinary you were. Your songs
Like the cat in Tenniel's *Alice* hung in air.
I saw you in a dream at Edinburgh Zoo
Conducting the indifferent rhinoceri,
Unmuscular Tarzan with a tuning fork.
The ivory cutlery found in your effects
Reiterating in a way I guess
James Joyce's cork-framed photographs of Cork
And Auden's take on verse's unsuccess.

Vivie

"We've had our medication now. The norm
Obtains. But what's the meaning? Who can tell?
What are the rules ? What is that uniform?
Where are the sheets I took from the hotel?

I think a rat eats T.S. Eliot's heart."
She wrote, and wept. When tears and ink had dried
She knew it for a thought that wouldn't start.
The entry ended where the dream had died.

"I know that somewhere in the arid grasses
One's reason's leaning skeleton remains.
My past's a snowstorm from a train that passes,
A glacier defaced with menstrual stains.

I see the stars trapped in the ilex tree
And cold Orion weep hot tears for me."

Stevie

Just let me recheck the date.
It is a woman's privilege, is it not, to be late?
Yes, as I feared, my library books are overdue
And I am too.
Yes, so too am I.
And like the sibyl at Cumea I would that I could die.

Standing Still

Sam with his saintsface
And frightened heart
Eulenspectator in the wind
On fire with Powers
And words hissing like the rain
On the chestnutsellers' braziers
At Kilometre Zero.

More Light

An inner ocean whispers in the shell
Unheard, until we raise it to the ear.
Seeds in the wind contain the flower bell.
The days accumulate. Another year
And so much tentative or unbegun,
Colour and brush potential aquarelles;
The sonnet sleeping in the fountain pen
Accuse us, and though all's to do again
Fine things in days to come will yet be done.
Who, midnight born, anticipates the sun?

Speed

Everyone dies at a different speed.
You live until someone discovers you dead.
Living is terribly strange indeed,
But dying is stranger, I hear it said.

Everyone dies at a different speed.
Every single gets multiple choices.
One wrote in dust what none may read
(He do the police in different voices).
Surprised the snake was rigid and warm
Eve receiving the gardener's seed
Came to terms with coming to term.
Everyone dies at a different speed.

Everyone dies at a different speed.
One said, 'Evil be thou my good.'
Another embraced a different creed,
Turned water to wine, and wine to blood,
So they hung him up on a cross to bleed.
Whatever you sow you're going to reap.
Living's expensive but dying is cheap.
Everyone dies at a different speed.

Wild Life in Suburbia

The sprinklers shimmer, and the mower ejects
Grasshalms in blurs, a shower of virid blades.
Snapdragons drowse above bright violets.
'Popeye the Sailor' irritates and fades.
On afternoons as dull as Labradors
Someone plays piano chords incessantly.
Spring surges through the suburbs like the sea,
The hawthorn foaming in a white neap tide.
Under the chestnut's trembling canopy
The radio announces an offside.

Lives

My father's cheek is rough.
I stand on wooden bricks to kiss him.
He is thirty-seven. I am six.

My mother's cheek is cheesecloth,
Soft as brie.
I stoop to kiss her.
I am fifty-six. She's eighty-three.

How old am I, my darling ? Always eighteen,
Remembering our kisses in between.

On My New Toshiba

Web is a wake where world's ideas mesh.
A neural engine idling in the dark
Until we boot it up. Where 'woof' will warp
Into 'mrgknao', and the words made flash
And fuse in iridescent indecision,
In bright eternities of evanescence.
Heaven without the beatific vision,
Analogue of our unplanned obsolescence.

The supernovae of the dreaming mind
Written in water, written on the wind,
Because, for all my sessions at the screen
Summoning up the sacred or profane,
For all my modem's myriad-minded choices
Its cursor can't call up my parents' voices.

Bagpipe Muzak

Daisy Duck's in Buchenwald,
Porky Pig's in Belsen,
Old Betj, gone in the teeth,
Is vomiting into the Elsan.
It's no go 'Die Fledermaus',
It's no go Picasso,
All we want is a sandwich
Made of Trebor mints and Brasso.

Jug the hare or let it sit,
Bin the cracked protractor.
If the costume wilna fit
Hire another actor.
It's no go down memory lane,
It's no go down Moses,
But go down on Dolores daughter of pain,
And you're sorted for wine and roses.

It's no go down to the sea again,
It's no go this send up,
And we're hurtling hard to the breaker's yard
Where all the Ladas end up.

La Nausée

I'm sick of Giacometti, Donezetti, Ferlinghetti, Alphabetti
Spaghetti, and you can shut the Serengeti for all I care.
I'm sick of tweets, Keats, the Beats, certain half-deserted streets
and what goes on between your sheets (however indiscreet).
I'm sick of stand-up straight men, sit down funnymen, fall
down drunk men, Donal Lunneymen, Umberto Eco
and the Bunnymen,
James Liddymen, and Ken Dodd and the fucking Diddymen.
I'm sick of chickens coming home to roost, Marcel Proust, wall-
to-wall carpeting and Walter Mitty.
And while you're at it you can stick *Fair City* where the sun
don't shine.
And anything you have to say about candleabra, Lady Gaga,
the extinction of the Quagga or *The Forsyte Saga* is going
straight in the Aga.
From Andrea Dworkin these boots were made for walkin'.
And if that sounded like Sinatra, no one calls me Nancy boy,
alright?
Thank you. Goodnight.

Haiku

Corrugated red
Roof in the snowfield's corner —
The postman's cottage.

Jaws

Encountering the corpse stiff in the trap,
This scrap whose mousecrap fouled my pots and pans,
I stoop to throw him out.
His bloodied snout
Sets me the question how (to coin a phrase)
My best laid plans are getting on these days.

No Lasting City

Now the taps are draped, the wounding
Awareness everything is winding
Down. Slow loss of understanding.
Words half grasped uncomprehending.

Pissing here the view I take's
Nothing lasts of what we make.
William Shakespeare, William Blake,
Melt like this urinal cake.

Milton's marble, Villon's snow,
'Have yez got no homes to go
To?' fade as must fade every rhyme.
HURRY UP! IT'S GONE THE TIME!

Cú na Mara

Headsick with hindsight, sun intensified
Swans bright as aspirin grate harsher than starch
On gritraw eyes, bob on an oily tide
Optical migraine, midday, Spanish Arch.

His heart trip hammering, he sees no charity
In the hard faces of the idling cops.
Forces a shaking angularity
Through Eyre Square's airheads, crusties, slobs and flops.

The train is moving, memories in the mind
Tumble like stormclouds in a gathering wind.

In a Dry Month

Try verse another way,
Try to get pissed less.
The list is endless
But the end is listless.
This too will pass.
Glass, bottle. Bottle, glass.
The grip grows limper,
Another drink for Auld Lang
Syne. Another bang. Another whimper.

'Freshen your drink?'
The barman asks. I blink
Awake. Earlier than I think.
Through glass in this
Locked room upstairs
One sees, not hears,
Birds begin day,
And, afterwards,
The Chaplain say
A prayer,
For whom?
That's neither here, nor there.
And anyway
Here's tea, and a nurse with a spray
To freshen the air.

Standing Still

The future all behind you now, what loss?
What odds in the heel of the hunt
What the gods have done to you?
Who gives a toss?
The stout in front of you
Won't kill you.
4:30 Rosie O Grady's, Harold's Cross,
And you still on the right side of the moss.

Here Endeth the Lesson

Tired birds from tree to tree are passing notes.
The cypress whispers dubious anecdotes.
The blackboard night gleams in the glantóir rain.
The bell rings but the moon is late again.
'Who?' asks the screech owl *cigire* passing by.
No merit stars hang in the classroom sky.
The flowers droop, the years wipe clean the slate.
But Sister Five Wounds' gravestone sits up straight.

Tricky Ole Gat

Teal go, bluer than noon by drowning owl
In tropic tree as I absorb gelato
Colum-indifferent to Gael or Gall
Or troubadour's inelegant legato.

For I've got ale and cakes by candlelight
And if time's tao gel ill, well what of that?
I'll play tag leo late into the night
Shaping strange statues sailors ogle at.

O aglet clicking at a lace's end
Cause not Hell's gale to blow away my hat
But let me meet at loge, or box, my friend,
El Gato lunico, Felix the cat.

And should the hour go late, I'll cry with puss,
'Lo! Gate of heaven, open unto us.'

Mature

Ah maun admit on evidence
Ma verse displays the influence
O' Burns frae Ayr.
But open T.S. Eliot's morgue,
His corpus is a smorgasbord.
O' Webster, Ford,
Twa Corbières,
And ain Laforgue.

ROYGBIV

Sun shines through rain today.
From Montparnasse it slants down
On church, atelier,
Café and cabaret —
Oh ladies look away
As Rimbaud with his pants down
Pisses an arc-en-ciel.

Wings

The sort of hat Magritte might wear,
Time-tarnished in the junk shop there;
With plumbeous wings that cannot fly,
Bronzini-buttocked Mercury
No godly augury can bring
To these dry shells and bottled ships;
Around our ankles, bickering
The pigeons pick at last night's chips.

Ingres-crimson backdrop, greasy chromo,
Someone's 'Susanna and the Elders',
An open-hearted 'Ecce Homo',
Stained Struwelpeter, Hans-in-Kelder,
Piano pushing sisyphi
(Embowlered Stan and Ollie) by
An alabaster Rodin's 'Kiss',
A cobweb-covered driving mirror
Reflecting us.
Reflect on this:

If pigeons, when they will, can fly
That mingle at the statue's base
With trippers at the Samothrace,
Whose is the winged victory?

Tender Buttons

How red Nicole is turning
Au supermarché St. Sulpice
Between the butter and the bacon counter
Under the checkout gaze of dyke Denise.
A Sappho burning in the aisles of grease.

Snapshot

The young girls, laughing, plait their hair
And sun their pierced mid-sections.
The lions in the London square,
Muscular, iron, unaware,
Stare off in four directions.

Dawnfhocail

Cockerel of the unrusty beak
A matin prayer to God you speak,
From spartan perch you praise Him high
While warm for shame in bed I lie.

Bán Again

On all the things I doubt or think
My little cat upset the ink.
Though sinless one I cannot scold you,
O Felix culpable I hold you.

Tigh Hughes

A ballad older than the famine
Sung for a girl by a blind man.
Hands that have never touched a woman
Squeeze love from an accordian.

Hangover 1

Bad as one feels
Between the jigs and the reels,
The absolute whore's
Betweeen the jigs and the cure.

Hangover 2

Stumbling into the front room from the pitch
Dark bedroom, having overslept till one,
I curse the glare — electric light's a bitch —
And find I'm trying to switch off the sun.

Death

A phone rang at 4:23
A.M. In a child's room full of alcoholics.
So the news of your passing came to me
Through Barney the Dinosaur's bollocks.

Porridge

I'm not that pushed about life or rhyme.
In fact when push comes to shove
I quite fancy easeful death from time to time
But I wouldn't call it love.

Feathers in the Wind

Hope springs eternal
In the kindling vernal.
But it comes to dust.
Oh doesn't it just?

Brass Tacks

Every even, every morn,
Every rising, every setting,
Yeats' crime of being born
And Beckett's worse crime of begetting.

Block

The candle flickers, and the shadow grows
Enormous as it dies. The room's too hot.
The streetlight's amber makes the fallen snow
A mezzotint of charcoal ocelot.

The dolcelatte moon emerges cold
Above the city that the clouds have made
Suddenly bright; its walls of blue and gold
Put everything I've written in the shade.

The Tortoiseshell that clutched the curtain rings
To this false summer has awakened now,
Angles the dusty rainbows of his wings.
Is my self-metaphor the melting snow?

No. Here's the image I've been seeking, plain,
The butterfly beating against the pane.

Cross Words

Look down on earth, oh King of infinite space,
Attend your son, hung on a strange device,
And the three figures kneeling at its base
Petitioning your blessing, on the dice.

Philosophy

Life's mostly balls, you know. And then one croaks.
Tall oaks from little acorns grow. Oaks fall.
    And that's all folks.